1/12

DATE DUE

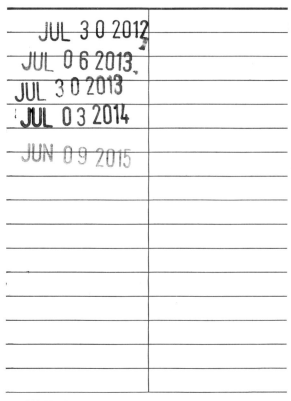
BRODART, CO.   Cat. No. 23-221

Summer
Colors

Brian Enslow

Enslow Elementary
an imprint of

Enslow Publishers, Inc.
40 Industrial Road
Box 398
Berkeley Heights, NJ 07922
USA

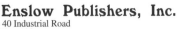

http://www.enslow.com

Enslow Elementary, an imprint of Enslow Publishers, Inc.

Enslow Elementary® is a registered trademark of Enslow Publishers, Inc.

Copyright © 2012 by Enslow Publishers, Inc.

Library of Congress Cataloging-in-Publication Data
Enslow, Brian.
    Summer colors / Brian Enslow.
        p. cm. — (All about colors of the seasons)
    Includes bibliographical references and index.
    Summary: "Learn about colors while looking at pictures of summer"— Provided by publisher.
    ISBN 978-0-7660-3907-0
    1. Summer—Juvenile literature. 2. Color—Juvenile literature. I. Title.
    QB637.6.E57 2012
    508.2—dc23   2011014449
Paperback ISBN: 978-1-59845-266-2

Printed in the United States of America

052011 Lake Book Manufacturing, Inc., Melrose Park, IL

10 9 8 7 6 5 4 3 2 1

To Our Readers: We have done our best to make sure all Internet Addresses in this book were active and appropriate when we went to press. However, the author and the publisher have no control over and assume no liability for the material available on those Internet sites or on other Web sites they may link to.

✪ Enslow Publishers, Inc., is committed to printing our books on recycled paper. The paper in every book contains 10% to 30% post-consumer waste (PCW). The cover board on the outside of each book contains 100% PCW. Our goal is to do our part to help young people and the environment too!

Photo Credits: 2happy/Shutterstock.com, p. 14; Daniel Padavona/Shutterstock.com, p. 22; Hallgerd/Shutterstock.com, p. 4; Irin-k/Shutterstock.com, p. 1, 6; Julie Phipps/Shutterstock.com, p. 16; Ketsu/Shutterstock.com, p. 21; Max777/Shutterstock.com, p. 18; Tarczas/Shutterstock.com, p. 20; Triff/Shutterstock.com, p. 10; Vaclav Volrab/Shutterstock.com, p. 12; Viktar Malyshchyts/Shutterstock.com, p. 8.

Cover Photo: Orla/Shutterstock.com.

Note to Parents and Teachers

Help pre-readers get a jumpstart on reading. These simple texts introduce new concepts with repetition of words and short simple phrases. Photos and illustrations fill the pages with color and effectively enhance the text. Free Educator Guides are available for this series at www.enslow.com. Search for the **All About Colors of the Seasons** series by name.

Contents

Words to Know

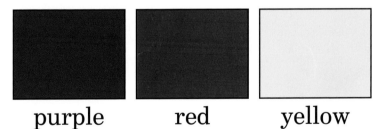

purple   red   yellow

rainbow of colors

red bug

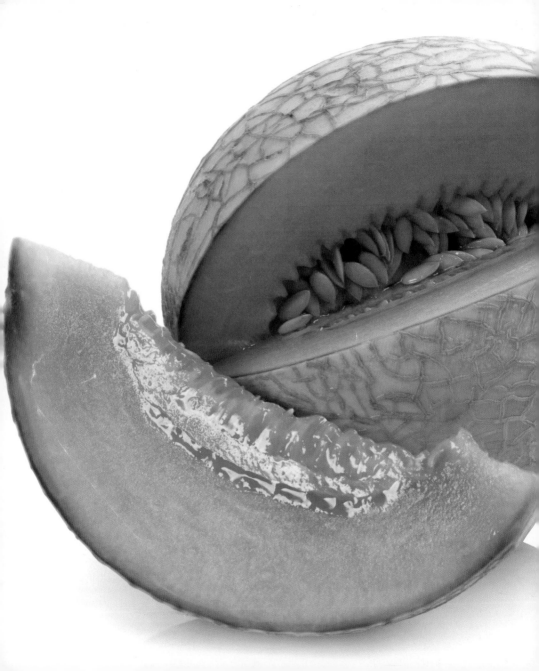

orange fruit

yellow flowers

green grass

blue sky

purple flower

brown mud

white flower

black glasses

What colors do you see?

Happy 4th of July!

Read More

Eckart, Edana. *Watching the Seasons*. New York, NY: Children's Press. 2004.

Mueller, Gerda. *Summer*. Edinburgh, UK: Floris Books. 2004.

Web Sites

KidsGeo
<http://www.kidsgeo.com/geography-for-kids/0017-the-earths-movements.php>

KidZone
<http://www.kidzone.ws/science/colorwheel.htm>

Index

Guided Reading Level: **B**
Guided Reading Leveling System is based on the guidelines recommended by Fountas and Pinnell.

Word Count: 30